From Belfast to Narnia:

THE LIFE *and* FAITH *of* C.S. LEWIS

TREMENDOUS LEADERSHIP
Leadership with a kick!

Life-Changing Classics, Volume XX

From Belfast to Narnia:

THE LIFE *and* FAITH *of* C.S. LEWIS

The C.S. Lewis Institute

From Belfast to Narnia:
The Life and Faith of C.S. Lewis

Published by Tremendous Leadership
PO Box 267
Boiling Springs, PA 17007
717-701-8159
www.tremendousleadership.com

ISBN: 978-1-936354-54-2

Cover Design: Karen Webb

First Edition

Printed in the United States of America

Table of Contents

PART TWO

PART THREE

Foreword from the Publisher

By Tracey C. Jones

C.S. Lewis (1898-1963) left an indelible mark upon the psyche of the English-speaking world of the 20th century. Works that he seeded into the soil of his generation were but the firstfruits of a greater harvest yet to come.

What was it about author Clive Staples Lewis that so resonated with people that even in the 21st century his name is a household word? Was it his friendship with J.R.R. Tolkien, author of *The Lord of the Rings*? Was it his mother's early training of Lewis or later his sorrow at her death that ignited his pen and enlightened modern day minds? Was it his intellectual curiosity about God or his faith in Him that drove Lewis to pen such books as *The Chronicles of Narnia, The Screwtape Letters*, and *Mere Christianity*?

The works of C.S. Lewis engage the reader in that eternal war for the soul. One cannot miss the divine orchestration that unfolds in Lewis's timeless series of writings. His work changed the way readers viewed good, evil, God, and the world, and have made us all better people.

Tremendous Leadership is honored to publish this brief but meaningful rendering of the life, faith, and ideas of one of the 20th century's most outstanding leaders, C.S. Lewis.

"I believe in Christianity as I believe that the sun has risen: not only because I see it, but because by it I see everything else."

C.S. Lewis, from his essay, *Is Theology Poetry?*

"If I find in myself a desire which no experience in this world can satisfy, the most probable explanation is that I was made for another world."

C.S. Lewis, *Mere Christianity*

"Faith, in the sense in which I am here using the word, is the art of holding on to things your reason has once accepted, in spite of your changing moods."

C.S. Lewis, *Mere Christianity*

Introduction

Clive Staples Lewis, better known as "Jack" to his friends and family, made only a few trips outside of his homeland, Great Britain, and yet today he is known globally as one of the greatest minds of the 20th century. His thirty plus books and countless essays cover a wide range of genres including science fiction, literary criticism, children's fiction, poetry, and Christian apologetics. He continues to have annual book sales in the millions around the world.

Lewis is probably best known for his children's books, *The Chronicles of Narnia,* which have been made into Hollywood films grossing hundreds of millions of dollars. Yet his wit, wisdom, and communications skills also made him the second best-known radio voice on the BBC after Winston Churchill during World War II. His "Broadcast Talks" to the British people on the Christian faith were eventually adapted into book form and retitled *Mere Christianity.* This book was named the most influential Christian book of the 20th century by the magazine, *Christianity Today*.

Not only was Lewis a gifted author and communicator, but he was also a committed friend who inspired others to share their gifts with the world. J.R.R. Tolkien, author of *The Hobbit* and *The Lord of the Rings*, credited his dear friend, Jack, as the one who encouraged him to continue writing and to publish these literary classics which have become household names.

C.S. Lewis died in 1963 on the same day that President John F. Kennedy was assassinated. And yet, more than half a century later, Lewis continues to grow in popularity as his keen intellect, rich imagination, and prophetic voice speak to the hearts and minds of both young and old in our 21st century world.

I'm grateful to Tracey Jones, the daughter of Charlie "Tremendous" Jones, who proposed the idea of publishing a summary of the life, faith, and ideas of C.S. Lewis to be included in the Life-Changing Classics series of Tremendous Leadership. Along with thousands of others, Tracey and I share a love for the writings of C.S. Lewis and are grateful for the way in which he lived his life in humble service to others and for the glory of God. I hope this introduction into the world and works of C.S. Lewis will spark your curiosity, and you will begin reading books like *Mere Christianity* and *The Chronicles of Narnia*. If you do, you may find yourself going "further up and further in" as you try to discover Who inspired one of the greatest writers of the 20th century.

Dr. Joel S. Woodruff
President of
The C.S. Lewis Institute

"A young man who wishes to remain a sound atheist cannot be too careful of his reading."

C.S. Lewis, *Surprised by Joy*

"Christianity is a statement which, if false, is of no importance, and if true, of infinite importance. The one thing it cannot be is moderately important."

C.S. Lewis, *God in the Dock*

—PART ONE—

The Life and Faith of C.S. Lewis

By Dr. Lyle Dorsett

"I'm tall, fat, rather bald, red-faced, double-chinned, black-haired, have a deep voice, and wear glasses for reading," C.S. Lewis wrote to a young admirer in 1954. If the famous author had been prone to notice clothing, he might have added that his trousers were usually in dire need of pressing, his jackets threadbare and blemished by snags and food spots, and his shoes scuffed and worn at the heels.

But Jack, as C.S. Lewis's friends knew him, was not bothered by fashion. It is not that he was slovenly. On the contrary, he was meticulous about the precise use of words, the quality of evidence presented in arguments, and the meter in verse. Nevertheless, the style and condition of personal attire were near the bottom of his list of concerns whereas books and ideas were among his top priorities.

Early Influences

Lewis was born into a bookish family of Protestants in Belfast, Ireland, on November 29, 1898. His father, Albert, and his mother, Florence Augusta Hamilton, possessed first-rate minds. They were members of the Church of Ireland. Eclectic in their reading tastes, they purchased and read many books, and their love for the printed word was passed on to their children. Jack and Warren (his only sibling, three years his senior) were not only read to aloud and taught to read, they were also encouraged to use the large family library.

In his autobiography, *Surprised by Joy*, C.S. Lewis recalled early memories of "endless books… There were books in the study, books in the dining room, books in the cloakroom, books (two deep) in the great bookcase on the landing, books in a bedroom, books piled as high as my shoulder in the cistern attic, books of all kinds." None of those books were off limits to him. On rainy days—and there were many in northern Ireland—he pulled volumes off the shelves and entered into worlds created by authors such as Conan Doyle, E. Nesbit, Mark Twain, and Henry Wadsworth Longfellow.

After brother Warnie was sent off to boarding school in England, Jack became somewhat reclusive. He spent more time in books and in an imaginary world of "dressed animals" and "knights in armor." But he did more than read books. He wrote and illustrated his own stories as well.

If Warren Lewis's exile across the Irish Sea to school in 1905 drove Jack further into himself and books, his mother's death from cancer in 1908 made him even more withdrawn. Mrs. Lewis's death came just three months prior to Jack's tenth birthday, and the young man was hurt deeply by her passing. Not only did he lose a mother, his father never fully recovered from her death. For many years afterward, both boys felt estranged from their father, and home life was never warm and satisfying again. The death of Mrs. Lewis convinced young Jack that the God he encountered in church and in the Bible his mother gave him was, if not cruel, at least a vague abstraction.

Four or five years later, by 1911 or 1912, and with the additional influence of a spiritually unorthodox boarding school matron,

Lewis forsook Christianity and became an avowed atheist.

By the autumn of 1914 C.S. Lewis was somewhat adrift. He had lost his faith and his mother, and he felt alienated from his father. He was extremely close to his brother, but they saw one another only on holidays. A new friendship was beginning with a fellow student, Arthur Greeves, but it was interrupted in September when C.S. Lewis was sent to Great Bookham, Surrey, to be privately tutored by W.T. Kirkpatrick, a brilliant teacher and friend of Lewis's father.

"The Great Knock," as the Lewis family dubbed Mr. Kirkpatrick, had a profound effect upon the teenage youth. He introduced Lewis to the classics in Greek, Latin, and Italian literature and helped him make a beginning in German. Kirkpatrick not only led Lewis to great books, he pushed him to understand them in the original languages.

A most demanding tutor, Kirkpatrick helped Jack learn how to criticize and analyze, and he taught him how to think, speak, and write logically. Consequently, after nearly three years with Kirkpatrick, C.S. Lewis was tough-minded and widely read. Many years later, Lewis wrote in *Surprised by Joy*, "My debt to him is very great, my reverence to this day undiminished."

The debt was large indeed. Kirkpatrick helped the young man prepare for scholarship examinations at Oxford, and the demanding mentor played no small role in Lewis's outstanding performance at University College where he took highest honors in honor moderations, greats, and English in 1920, 1922, and 1923.

If Kirkpatrick taught Lewis to think critically and to demand evidence for even the most casual assertions, Oxford introduced him to a wide horizon of ideas. Whereas Lewis's hard-pressing mentor had helped him reinforce his atheism, a few associates at Oxford forced him to reexamine his belief in a universe without God.

Oxford Years

Lewis entered the world of Oxford in 1917 as a student, and he never really left. Despite an interruption to fight in World War I and his professorship at Cambridge, beginning in 1955, he always maintained his home and friends in Oxford. He loved the bookshops, the pubs, and the Bodleian Library, and he reveled in the company of local men who loved to read, write, and discuss books. His attachment to Oxford was so strong that when he taught at Cambridge from 1955 to 1963, he commuted back to Oxford on weekends so that he could be close to familiar places and beloved friends.

It was in Oxford that Lewis pursued things of the mind with fervor. Ideas, books, and debates were ordinary fare in this heady environment. With no particular purpose in life beyond stimulating his imagination, feeding his intellectual curiosity, and writing for publication and posterity, he thoroughly enjoyed academic life. In 1919 he published his first book, a cycle of lyrics entitled *Spirits in Bondage,* which he wrote under the pseudonym Clive Hamilton. In 1924 he became a philosophy tutor at University College.

Then in 1925 he was elected a fellow of Magdalen College where he tutored in English language and literature. The next year his second volume of poetry, *Dymer,* was published under the name Clive Hamilton.

Alongside the generally self-centered life Lewis was leading, he demonstrated a loyal and generous nature. When his college roommate, Paddy Moore, was killed in World War I, Jack befriended Paddy's mother, Mrs. Janie King Moore, and her adolescent daughter Maureen. Then in 1920, after completing his first degree, Lewis decided to share lodgings with them so that he could more carefully look out for their needs.

Spiritual Awakening

This gesture of kindness did more than help Mrs. Moore and Maureen; it moved C.S. Lewis outside of himself and taught him patience. The association with the Moores also introduced him to Mrs. Moore's brother, a combat veteran who suffered from a severe war-inflicted nervous disorder. This personal encounter apparently shook Lewis's confidence in materialism because a letter he wrote in 1923 to his friend Arthur Greeves suggests a slight spiritual awakening. It seems that the "Doc," as the Moores and Lewis referred to him, came to stay with the trio for three weeks. During the visit "Doc" underwent an ordeal of extreme mental torture. After the attack, when the poor wretch was hospitalized, Lewis wrote to his friend that "Doc" had believed he was in Hell. He wore out his body in the "awful mental tortures" and then died from heart failure— "unconscious at the end, thank God." Lewis concluded his observation by suggesting it is "a damned world—and we once thought we could be happy with books and music!"

The spiritual awakening continued, enhanced by reading books by George MacDonald and G.K. Chesterton. One MacDonald volume called *Phantastes* had a powerful impact on his thinking. "What it actually did to me," wrote Lewis, "was to convert, even to baptize... my imagination." At Oxford Lewis continued to read MacDonald, and he imbibed G.K. Chesterton as well. The latter author's books, especially *The Everlasting Man*, raised serious questions about the young intellectual's materialism.

While MacDonald and Chesterton were stirring Lewis's thoughts, a close friend, Owen Barfield, with whom he spent much time during and after their student years, pounced on the logic of Jack Lewis's atheism. Barfield was an atheist who became a Christian. He frequently badgered Lewis about his materialism. So did Nevill Coghill, a fellow student and lifelong friend who was brilliant, yet he was, to Lewis's amazement, "a Christian and a thorough-going supernaturalist."

Soon after joining the English faculty at Magdalen College, Lewis met two more Christians, Hugo Dyson and J.R.R. Tolkien. These men became close friends of Lewis. He admired their brilliance and their logic. Soon Lewis recognized that most of his friends, like his favorite authors—MacDonald, Chesterton, Johnson, Spenser, and Milton—held to this Christian angle of vision which threatened his whole world view.

Gradually during the 1920s, two paths were converging in Lewis's mind: one was reason, the other intuition. In 1929 these roads met, and C.S. Lewis surrendered and admitted that "God was God, and [I] knelt and prayed." Within two years the reluctant convert admitted that Jesus Christ is the Son of God—God Incarnate. With this revelation the Oxford don became a communicant in the Church of England.

A New Life

Christian history shows that when men and women meet Jesus, recognize His nature, and then decide to trust and follow Him, they become strikingly different people. Those who convert, who turn around and obey Christ's command to "follow me," are clearly people with changed lives. If evidence of conversion is a new life, C.S. Lewis was obviously a believer after 1931. Many changes were apparent. His life took on a new purpose—to know and obey God.

This came to fruition most demonstrably in his writing. Earlier efforts to become a poet were laid to rest. The new Christian devoted his talent and energy to writing prose that reflected his recently found faith. Within two years of his conversion Lewis published *The Pilgrim's Regress: An Allegorical Apology for Christianity, Reason and Romanticism.* This little volume opened a thirty-year stream of books on Christian apologetics and discipleship that became a lifelong avocation. Between 1933 and his death in 1963, C.S. Lewis wrote books, including the seven-volume *Chronicles of Narnia*, *The Screwtape Letters*, *The Great Divorce*, and *Mere Christianity*, that nudged atheists and agnostics toward Christian faith and encouraged and nurtured believers.

As a good steward and responsible professional, Lewis did not ignore his academic discipline. He wrote literary history and criticism such as *The Allegory of Love: A*

Study in Medieval Tradition, *Rehabilitations and Other Essays*, and *English Literature in the Sixteenth Century Excluding Drama*. These books are still widely read and highly regarded.

Despite the large quantity and high quality of his academic publications, Lewis became known as a literary evangelist. The tone and impact of his theological and apologetical books help account for this reputation, as did his own assertion in a rejoinder to his critic, Dr. W.N. Pittenger, published in *The Christian Century*, November 26, 1958, where Lewis admitted that most of what he wrote "is evangelistic."

A Growing Reputation

If Christianity altered Lewis's writing habits, the publication of those books had a palpable effect on his personal life. First of all, the change was manifested in the mail. Once Lewis's books became popular, which they did by the 1940s, he was inundated by letters. Because the famous author believed it was God's will for him to answer most of this mail himself and because he was convinced, as he said in "The Weight Of Glory," that there are "no ordinary people," he took time to write with care to each correspondent regardless of age, education, or place in society. This enterprise consumed many hours each week.

Furthermore, life with fame was laden with other pressures. There were numerous invitations to entertain guests, grant interviews, give lectures, and preach sermons. Writing, to be sure, is a lonely enterprise. This Lewis understood. And even though he felt called by God to write, he likewise felt it was required of him to counsel those who made the pilgrimage to The Kilns, his home on the edge of Oxford. Frequently, he believed it was his calling to explain the Christian faith to people over BBC radio and to airmen at RAF bases during World War II.

Preaching sermons, giving talks, and expressing his theological views over the radio throughout the United Kingdom bolstered Lewis's reputation and increased his book sales. With these new circumstances came other changes—not the least being a marked upswing in annual income. Throughout the 1920s Lewis had been getting by on little money. During his student years his father provided an allowance, and Jack supplemented that in various ways. Nevertheless, money was always scarce. And when the young academician took on the responsibility for Mrs. Moore and her daughter, finances were always tight even with the regular tutorial stipend.

As book royalties mounted during the later 1940s and continued to spiral upward thereafter, C.S. Lewis refused to upgrade his standard of living. Partly out of disdain for conspicuous living but mostly out of commitment to Jesus Christ, he established a charitable fund for his royalty earnings. Neither the extent nor the recipients of C.S. Lewis's charity are fully known. Indeed, he made valiant efforts to conceal this information. It is known that he supported numerous impoverished families, underwrote education fees for orphans and poor seminarians, and put money into scores of charities and church ministries.

A Late Marriage

The outreach of Lewis's books and the impact of his charity conspired to make still another significant change in his lifestyle. During the last decade of his earthly pilgrimage, Lewis's world was invaded by an American woman and her two children. In the autumn of 1952 Joy Davidman Gresham, who had become a Christian partly because she read *The Great Divorce* and *The Screwtape Letters*, visited her spiritual mentor in England. Soon after, her husband abandoned her for another woman. In the meantime, the divorcee, a writer in her own right, moved to London with her two adolescent boys, David and Douglas.

Joy Davidman Gresham gradually fell into financial trouble. Her acquaintance with C.S. Lewis led to his underwriting the boarding school education of David and Douglas. From charity and common literary interests grew a deep friendship, and eventually *agape* became *eros*. They were married in 1956.

Joy was sixteen years Lewis's junior, but that did not prevent a happy marriage. A savage case of cancer, however, cut short their life together. After several years of reprieve from an earlier and nearly fatal bout with cancer, Joy Lewis passed away in Oxford on July 13, 1960.

Joy's entry into Jack's life brought much happiness. As he wrote to one friend soon after their marriage, "It's funny having at 59 the sort of happiness most men have in their twenties... 'Thou has kept the good wine till now'." Joy brought C.S. Lewis love, companionship, and two stepsons, complete with all of the delights and problems that naturally come in such circumstances. Furthermore, Mrs. Lewis brought insights, ideas, and a new angle of vision. Raised in a Jewish home and having written a book on the Ten Commandments, *Smoke on the Mountain,* she encouraged him to renew his writing of apologetics, in particular *Reflections on the Psalms.* Her influence on what Jack considered his best book, *Till We Have Faces,* was so profound that he told one close friend she was actually his coauthor.

Critics Emerge

C.S. Lewis's marriage to Joy Davidman did not enhance his reputation in Great Britain.

Long assumed to be a confirmed bachelor, the esteemed professor not only married late in life, but he married an American who was at once Jewish, divorced, and personally rather abrasive. In brief, the marriage did not set well with most of Mr. Lewis's friends and acquaintances. The critics notwithstanding, Jack's faithful brother Warren, who lived at The Kilns with Jack before, during, and after the years with Joy, supported him as did a few other close friends. C.S. Lewis was hurt by the disapproval of his old friends and colleagues, but it was by no means a new experience for him. Although he enjoyed the conviviality of weekly get-togethers with fellow Inklings (intellectuals and writers who met regularly to exchange ideas and share in good conversation) and the prodigious successes of his books, Lewis was frequently under attack for his decidedly Christian lifestyle. Close friends, among them Owen Barfield and J.R.R. Tolkien, openly disapproved of Lewis's evangelistic speaking and writing. And if the opprobrium of fellow believers was unpleasant, it was mild compared with the attacks from colleagues and strangers who did not share the Oxford author's faith.

It is common knowledge that Lewis's Christian books caused so much disapproval that he was more than once passed over for a professorship at Oxford with the honors going to men of lesser reputation. It was Magdalene College at Cambridge University that finally honored Lewis with a chair in 1955 and thereby recognized his original and important contributions to English literary history and criticism.

Along with Lewis's international reputation, ever-growing royalties, and thousands of fans throughout the English-speaking world came increasing alienation. Did Lewis take comfort in his Lord's warning in the Sermon on the Mount that his disciples would indeed be insulted and persecuted? We do not know.

Lewis died at The Kilns on November 22, 1963. He is buried in the cemetery of Holy Trinity Church, Headington Quarry, Oxford, beside his brother who lived ten more years. His letters and books, and the lives these writings touch, are his legacy.

"God is no fonder of intellectual slackers than He is of any other slacker."

C.S. Lewis, *Mere Christianity*

"To be a Christian means to forgive the inexcusable, because God has forgiven the inexcusable in you."

C.S. Lewis, *The Weight of Glory*

—PART TWO—

C.S. Lewis's Seven Key Ideas

By Dr. Art Lindsley

I have heard it said that many well-known thinkers have only two or three key ideas that they develop from various angles throughout their lives. It might be asked: What are C.S. Lewis's key ideas? I have chosen seven to summarize in this essay. The seven I have chosen are:

1. Chronological Snobbery
2. Desire

3. Imagination
4. Objective Values vs. Relativism
5. Myth
6. Immortality
7. Comprehensiveness

1. Chronological Snobbery

One obstacle that C.S. Lewis had to overcome was what he called his "chronological snobbery." By that he meant the assumption that whatever has gone out of date is thereby discredited. For instance, people might ask, "What does a 2,000-year-old faith have to do with me?" One of Lewis's friends helped him to ask about ideas that seemed outdated. Why did an idea go out of date, and was it ever refuted? If so, where, by whom, and how conclusively? C.S. Lewis later argued that reading old books helped provide a corrective to the blindness induced by our own age. We ought, he maintained, to read one old book for every new one or, if that's too much, then one old one for every three new ones. Otherwise, we may be easily enslaved to the ideas of the recent past.

2. *Desire*

C.S. Lewis believed that we were made for "joy." God is the great "hedonist." He provides things for humans to do all day long, like "sleeping, eating, drinking, making love, playing, praying, working." But, he also believed that to focus on these "second things" and neglect "first things," such as worshiping and loving God, was to be "too easily pleased." He wrote:

> *Our Lord finds our desires not too strong, but too weak. We are half-hearted creatures, fooling about with drink, sex, and ambition when infinite joy is offered us, like an ignorant child who wants to go on making mud pies in a slum because he cannot imagine what is meant by the*

offer of a holiday at the sea. We are far too easily pleased.

Lewis's argument for God's existence from the nature of our desires is fascinating and thought provoking. Just as the existence of hunger points to satisfaction in the reality of food, thirst in drink, sexual desire in sex, drowsiness in sleep, etc., so other "natural" desires: spiritual hunger, desire for supernatural encounters, aspirations to immortality, and so on, act as cosmic pointers to real supernatural satisfaction.

3. *Imagination*

C.S. Lewis viewed reason as the natural "organ of truth" and imagination as the "organ of meaning." He believed that the only way we grasp any idea with clarity is if we have an image associated with it. He was able to work with equal facility in philosophical arguments or in writing fiction. Lewis used images to illustrate his apologetics and communicated profound ideas in his fiction. For instance, he wrote a great critique of relativism in *Abolition of Man* and communicated the same ideas in the novel, *That Hideous Strength*.

Imagination acted as a cosmic pointer to Lewis. Once, during his years of unbelief, he was going on a train ride, so he bought a book to read, George MacDonald's *Phantastes*. While he was reading, he said that a "new quality" touched his life, and his imagination was "baptized." The quality was later described by Lewis to be "holiness." Although it took a while for the rest of him to catch up (reason—satisfied; will—submitted), it was an important first step. Having had this early experience, it is not surprising that he thought others might feel a similar thing. He felt his Narnia series might sneak past "watchful dragons" of religiosity, enabling his readers to see old things in new ways.

4. Absolutes vs. Relativism

C.S. Lewis argued for objective truth and morality against the relativism of his (and our) day. He felt that establishing the reality of truth and goodness was an essential preparation for the Gospel. He wrote:

> *For my part, I believe we ought to work not only at spreading the gospel (that certainly) but also at a certain preparation for the gospel. It is necessary to recall many to the Law of Nature before we talk about God. For Christ promises forgiveness of sins: But what is that to those who since they do not know the Law of Nature, do not know that they have sinned? Who will take the medicine unless he knows he is in the grip of disease? Moral relativity is the enemy we have to overcome before we tackle atheism.*

Lewis's arguments against relativism are set forth in *Mere Christianity* (Book I), *Abolition of Man*, and in numerous essays.

5. Myth

Early in C.S. Lewis's life he noticed the parallels between pagan myths and classic Christianity. In his education it was assumed that the pagan myths were false and Christianity true. Why was this—religion—and this one alone—true? This is one factor that led to his unbelief.

He resolved the problem and wrote about myth in a number of places. A key to his resolution was the increased understanding that if God created the world in a certain way and the human mind with a definite structure, it is not surprising that those patterns reoccur. The only question is, are any of these myths truer than others or, more precisely, are any of these myths also fact? He came to believe that Jesus was the "myth become fact."

Later he defined myth as an "unfocused gleam of divine truth falling on human imagination." Lewis discusses parallel mythologies in his book *Miracles*, his novel *Till We Have Faces*, and in other places.

6. Immortality

Walter Hooper, a C.S. Lewis scholar, argues that C.S. Lewis's central idea was that all people are immortal. Lewis wrote:

> *There are no ordinary people. You have never talked to a mere mortal. Nations, cultures, arts, civilizations—these are mortal, and their life is to ours as the life of a gnat. But it is immortals whom we joke with, work with, marry, snub and exploit—immortal horrors or everlasting splendors. This does not mean that we are to be perpetually solemn. We must play. But our merriment must be of that kind (and it is, in fact, the merriest kind)*

> *which exists between people who have, from the outset, taken each other seriously—no flippancy, no superiority, no presumption.*

Lewis manifested this belief by writing personally to everyone who wrote to him (usually handwritten letters) and by giving away all the proceeds of his books.

Hooper tells the story of a time when he was with Lewis, and they were talking about a man who was very boring. Hooper told Lewis that the man succeeded in interesting him by the very intensity of his boredom. Lewis replied, "Yes, but let us not forget that Our Lord might well have said, 'As ye have done it unto one of the least of these my bores, you have done it to me'." In fact, Lewis felt that it was sometimes his duty to visit and help such people.

Lewis also gives us glorious pictures of heaven. For instance, in my favorite of the *Narnia Chronicles*, *The Last Battle*, he portrays life in the higher country as infinite adventures with an infinitely creative God for all eternity. The last paragraph of *The Last Battle* says:

> *And for us this is the end of all the stories, and we can most truly say that they all lived happily ever after. But for them it was only the beginning of the real story. All their life in this world and all their adventures in Narnia had only been the cover and the title page: now at last they were beginning Chapter One of the Great Story which no one on earth has read: which goes on forever: in which every chapter is better than the one before.*

7. Comprehensiveness

C.S. Lewis believed that Jesus was the way, the truth, and the life and that all truth pointed to Him. Lewis said: "*I believe in Christianity as I believe the sun has risen not only because I see it, but because by it I see everything else.*"

He was influenced by G.K. Chesterton who maintained that we become convinced of a theory not just when something proves it but only when everything proves it. Lewis explored reason, imagination, fiction, non-fiction, art, philosophy, classic literature, and poetry, finding shafts of light and following them back to the sun (Son).

"Aim at Heaven and you will get earth 'thrown in:' aim at earth and you will get neither."

C.S. Lewis, *Mere Christianity*

"I am trying here to prevent anyone saying the really foolish thing that people often say about Him: 'I'm ready to accept Jesus as a great moral teacher, but I don't accept his claim to be God.' That is the one thing we must not say. A man who was merely a man and said the sort of things Jesus said would not be a great moral teacher. He would either be a lunatic—on a level with the man who says he is a poached egg — or else he would be the Devil of Hell. You must make your choice. Either this man was, and is, the Son of God: or else a madman or something worse. You can shut Him up for a fool, you can spit at Him and kill Him as a demon; or you can fall at His feet and call Him Lord and God. But let us not come with any patronising nonsense about His being a great human teacher. He has not left that open to us. He did not intend to."

C.S. Lewis, *Mere Christianity*

—PART THREE—

A C.S. Lewisian Invitation

By Dr. Randy Newman

I've read enough of C.S. Lewis's delightful writings to know that he'd be amazed that anyone would put together a book like this one. He suspected that he and all his work would be forgotten within five years of his death. He could not have been more wrong.

But once he got past the shock of a book about C.S. Lewis, he would express deep concern and exhort people to look past him and consider seriously the person, teaching, and work of Jesus. He would be appalled if people settled for "Mere C.S. Lewis" instead of "Mere Christianity."

If you've read this far in this publication, you know that the gospel of Jesus Christ dramatically changed C.S. Lewis. He would want you to experience that same kind of transformation and connect with a local church that believed the Bible as he did. He regularly called people to make a decision before time ran out in their lives. Lewis wrote in his classic book *Mere Christianity,*

> *It will be too late then to choose your side. There is no use saying you choose to lie down when it has become impossible to stand up. That will not be the time for choosing: it will be the time when we discover which side we really have chosen, whether we realized it before or not. Now, today,*

this moment, is our chance to choose the right side. God is holding back to give us that chance. It will not last for ever. We must take it or leave it.

Would you like to respond to Jesus and follow Him? Are you ready to place your trust in what He did on the cross as the payment for your sin? If so, you can pray now and ask Jesus to forgive you of your sins and to become the Lord and Savior of your life. He would be overjoyed if you did. As you consider this life changing (eternity changing!) decision, reflect on these words that Lewis wrote at the very end of *Mere Christianity.*

...there must be a real giving up of the self. You must throw it away 'blindly' so to speak... The principle runs through all life from top to bottom. Give up your self, and you will find your real self. Lose your life and you will save it. Submit to death,

> *death of your ambitions and favourite wishes everyday and death of your whole body in the end: submit with every fibre of your being, and you will find eternal life. Keep back nothing. Nothing that you have not given away will ever be really yours. Nothing in you that has not died will ever be raised from the dead. Look for yourself, and you will find in the long run only hatred, loneliness, despair, rage, ruin and decay. But look for Christ and you will find Him, and with Him everything else thrown in.*

If you have made this decision to give yourself to Jesus or if you would like to ask more questions about what it means to be a follower of Christ, we here at the C.S. Lewis Institute would be happy to talk with you. You may contact us at:

staff@cslewisinstitute.org

"You can't get a cup of tea large enough or a book long enough to suit me."

C.S. Lewis—
in a conversation with a friend

"Some day you will be old enough to start reading fairy tales again."

C.S. Lewis,
The Lion, the Witch and the Wardrobe

"Since it is so likely that children will meet cruel enemies, let them at least have heard of brave knights and heroic courage."

C.S. Lewis,
On Stories: And Other Essays on Literature

Suggested Reading *from the* Writings *of* C.S. Lewis

Children's Fiction

The Chronicles of Narnia (1950-1956)

Perhaps his most popular work, this series of seven fiction stories is written for children but loved by adults around the world. The adventures of Peter, Edmund, Susan, Lucy and others who are transported magically into the land of Narnia bring to light the struggle of good versus evil as Aslan, the Great Lion of Narnia, guides his people in the fight against the White Witch and the other dark forces in this kingdom. A number of the books from The Chronicles of Narnia have been turned into movies.

On Christian Faith

Mere Christianity (1952)

The magazine, *Christianity Today*, named this book the most influential Christian book of the 20th century. It is based on a series of radio broadcasts given by Lewis on the BBC radio to the British people during World War II. He makes the case for the truth and beauty of Christianity and offers an introduction into the essential or "mere" beliefs and means of living out the Christian faith.

The Screwtape Letters (1942)

First published as a series in a British newspaper, *The Screwtape Letters*, written in a creative and thoughtful way, gives readers insight into the devil's playbook for tempting and leading humans away from God. *The Screwtape Letters* is written as a collection of letters from a devil named Screwtape to his nephew Wormwood, a junior devil in training.

Science Fiction

The Space Trilogy: Out of the Silent Planet (1938); Perelandra: A Novel (1943); That Hideous Strength: A ModernFairy-Tale for Grown-Ups (1945)

This Orwellian-like series of stories finds the hero, Ransom, in a battle for truth and humanity against the mad scientist, Dr. Weston and others, as they travel to Mars, Venus, and other planets in outer space.

Autobiography

Surprised By Joy: The Shape of My Early Life (1955)

This spiritual autobiography of Lewis provides insight into the people, authors, and ideas that shaped him. It examines the highlights from his progressive spiritual journey which began with his Christian upbringing to atheism in his teens. Later, as an Oxford academic, following the brutalities of World War I, he began to search for truth in philosophy and the religions of pantheism and theism. Eventually through the witness of close friends, he came to believe in the truth and beauty of Christianity.

A Grief Observed (1961)

Following the death of Lewis's wife, Joy Davidman, Lewis was stricken with grief. He turned to the tool that had helped him work through problems in the past—the craft of writing. This cathartic journal describes in detail his questions and battle with grief in a raw and honest way. He initially published this work under a pseudonym, N.W. Clerk. It has inspired thousands of people since and has given them words and a voice for their feelings of grief following the loss of a loved one.

The C.S. Lewis Institute

The C.S. Lewis Institute was founded in 1976 and endeavors, in the legacy of C.S. Lewis, to develop disciples who will articulate, defend, and live their faith in Christ in personal and public life. From its inception the Institute has been interdenominational, has worked closely with a variety of churches, and sees itself as a servant ministry, assisting churches and pastors in making disciples of Jesus Christ. This takes the form of discipleship programs, evangelism and apologetics training, area-wide conferences/seminars, pastor fellowships, and resources in print and on the web.

Discipleship Resources

Reflections: A one-page monthly reflection on a thought or idea from C.S. Lewis, applicable to one's personal life. For more information please go to

www.cslewisinstitute.org/Reflections.

The Fellows Program: The Institute's flagship, year-long discipleship program designed for those who are ready to be intentional about spiritual growth in Christ, and who desire for God to use them in powerful ways for His Kingdom.

The Fellows Program's unique approach focuses on the integration of the heart and mind, and the connection of faith and vocation in an interdenominational setting, and is intentionally designed to dramatically alter the trajectory of spiritual growth to help Fellows become more and more like Jesus. A combination of dynamic teachers and classic writers, experienced mentors, effective small groups and active engagement in the Word aims to produce mature believers who can articulate, defend and joyfully live out their faith in every aspect of their lives. For more information please go to

www.cslewisinstitute.org/CSLI_Locations.

Heart & Mind Discipleship DVD and Study Guide: A 10-week small group discipleship program designed for anyone who wants to deepen their understanding of faith in Christ and focus on growing in Christ. For more information please go to

www.cslewisinstitute.org/products.

C·S· LEWIS INSTITUTE

Discipleship of Heart and Mind

8001 Braddock Road, Suite 301
Springfield, VA 22151
703-914-5602
cslewisinstitute.org

NOTES

NOTES

NOTES

NOTES

NOTES

NOTES

NOTES

NOTES

NOTES